SPORTING CHAMPIONSHIPS
Rose Bowl

Lauren Diemer

WEIGL PUBLISHERS INC.

Published by Weigl Publishers Inc.
350 5th Avenue, Suite 3304, PMB 6G
New York, NY 10118-0069

Website: www.weigl.com
Copyright ©2010 WEIGL PUBLISHERS INC.

Library of Congress Cataloging-in-Publication Data

Diemer, Lauren.
  Rose Bowl / Lauren Diemer.
      p. cm. -- (Sporting championships)
  Includes index.
  ISBN 978-1-60596-638-0 (hard cover : alk. paper) -- ISBN 978-1-60596-639-7 (soft cover : alk. paper)
  1. Rose Bowl (Football game)--Juvenile literature. I. Title.
  GV957.R6D54 2010
  796.332'630979493--dc22
                                    2009008362

Printed in China
1 2 3 4 5 6 7 8 9 0 13 12 11 10 09

Weigl acknowledges Getty Images as its primary image supplier for this title.

Project Coordinator
Heather C. Hudak

Design
Terry Paulhus

CONTENTS

4   What is the Rose Bowl?

6   Rose Bowl History

8   Rules of the Game

10 The Football Field

12 Football Equipment

14 Qualifying to Play

16 Where They Play

18 Mapping Rose Bowl Winners

20 Women in Football

22 Historical Highlights

24 Legends and Current Stars

26 Famous Firsts

28 The Rise of the Rose Bowl

30 Test Your Knowledge

31 Further Research

32 Glossary/Index

12

21

30

What is the Rose Bowl?

The Rose Bowl is a post-season game played between two of the best college football teams in the United States. It is played in Pasadena, California, on New Year's Day each year. If New Year's Day falls on a Sunday, the game is played on January 2nd. The Rose Bowl takes place in the afternoon in the warmth of California's winter sunlight.

The Rose Bowl was created as part of the Tournament of Roses. This tournament, known as "America's New Year Celebration," is a festival of flowers, music, and sporting events that has taken place on New Year's Day since 1890. The Rose Bowl was first played during the Tournament of Roses in 1902. After that first game, there was not another Rose Bowl game for 14 years. Since 1916, the Rose Bowl has been played every year.

At the 2009 Rose Bowl, Mark Sanchez of the USC Trojans passed for 413 yards (378 meters) and four touchdowns.

The Rose Bowl has been the most attended college football game in the United States since 1945. It has developed into one of the highest-attended sporting events in the country. In fact, the Rose Bowl has been sold out each year since 1947.

The Rose Bowl is the oldest **bowl game** played in the United States. It has been played for so many years that it has gained the nickname, "The Granddaddy of Them All."

CHANGES THROUGHOUT THE YEARS

PAST	PRESENT
There were few rules, and many players were injured during games.	Rules exist to help decrease the number of injuries.
The Rose Bowl was played at Pasadena's Tournament Park until 1923.	The Rose Bowl is played at the Rose Bowl Stadium.
Only one bowl game was played annually in the 1930s.	In 2008, 32 National Collegiate Athletic Association (NCAA) bowl games were played.

Rose Bowl Trophies

The Leishman Trophy was named after 1920 Tournament of Roses President William L. Leishman. He was responsible for the construction of the Rose Bowl Stadium. The Rose Bowl Game Trophy was designed and created by Tiffany & Co. It is made from about 16 pounds (7.3 kilograms) of silver and is almost 21 inches (53 centimeters) tall.

The Most Valuable Player (MVP) in each Rose Bowl receives a crystal trophy. This award was created in 1953 and was given **retroactively** to 1902. In a few cases, more than one player has received the crystal trophy. Beginning in 2005, a **defensive** and an **offensive** MVP were named for each Rose Bowl.

Rose Bowl History

In the early 1900s, football was becoming a popular sport with many Americans. Organizers of the Tournament of Roses thought hosting a major football event would be a great way to ring in the New Year. The Rose Bowl was originally titled the Tournament East-West Football Game. The first game was played in 1902, between Michigan University and California's Stanford University.

Michigan University's football team had been the top-ranked team during that football season. The team had won all 11 of the games it had played, and event organizers felt certain the team would draw a big crowd to watch the game. Stanford University had a strong team as well, but they were no match for the Michigan team. Stanford decided to stop playing in the third quarter. Michigan won the game with a score of 49 to 0.

The Michigan Wolverines have won seven national championships and 42 conference championships.

The Rose Bowl became the first college football game to be broadcast nationally in color and the first to broadcast live to many parts of the world. People across the country watch the game on television today.

The game was not the success the Tournament of Roses organizers had hoped it would be. As a result, they decided to focus on different events for the next 14 years. They held chariot races, ostrich races, and even a race between a giraffe and an elephant.

For the 1916 Tournament of Roses, organizers decided to host another football game. During this game, the State College of Washington defeated Brown University. With a final score of 14 to 0 for Washington, it was a more interesting game to watch than the 1902 game, when the scores were so far apart. The Rose Bowl has been played every year since.

The Rose Bowl has a halftime show between the second and third quarters. This usually involves live music and performances.

Rose Bowl Royalty

Every year, about 1,000 young women apply to become the Rose Bowl Queen. In September, finalists are judged on their poise, school achievements, public-speaking skills, and personalities. The winner and six runners up, or princesses, are chosen after one month of interviews. They ride on the Royal Court float in the Rose Bowl Parade and reign over the Rose Bowl Game. In addition, the queen and princesses attend events throughout the year to promote the Tournament of Roses.

Rules of the Game

Football has many rules that have developed and changed over the years. A number of these rules have been created to keep the players safe from injury.

1 Playing the Game

The goal of a football game is for a team to carry a ball into the opposing team's end zone. They do this by running with the ball and passing it from player to player. During the game, the offense has four chances, or downs, to move the ball 10 yards down the field. If the ball is moved 10 yards or more, the offense starts again at the first down. It has four more chances to move the ball at least another 10 yards. During this time, the defense tries to keep the offense from moving the ball ahead.

2 Line of Scrimmage

The line of scrimmage is where the two teams meet at the beginning of the play. At the **snap**, at least seven offensive players face the defending team on the line. Defending players are positioned to block the offensive team's players. Players not on the line of scrimmage must be at least 1 yard behind it.

3 Scoring Points

Points are scored when a team gets a touchdown, field goal, or conversion. A team gets a touchdown when one of its players carries the football to the end of the opposing team's side of the field. A touchdown is worth six points. After a touchdown, the scoring team can earn more points. This is called conversion. The ball can be kicked through the goalposts for one extra point, or carried into the end zone for two points. Conversion plays begin very close to the defending team's end zone. A field goal is scored when a kicker sends the ball through the goalposts. It is worth three points.

4 Offside

If a player moves before the snap of the ball, an offside penalty is called. Sometimes, a defensive player moves across the line of scrimmage and touches an offensive player or does not move back across the line of scrimmage before the play starts. That player's team is given a penalty and is moved back 5 yards on the field.

5 On the Clock

There are four quarters in a game of football. Each quarter is 15 minutes in length. It takes about three hours to play four 15-minute quarters. This is because the clock is stopped when there is a penalty or a play has ended.

Making the Call

Referees can be seen on the field wearing black and white striped shirts. They make sure the players are following all of the rules of the game. Referees determine if a player has scored a touchdown, gone out of bounds, or has committed a **foul**. If there is a "flag on the play," the referee has seen a rule being broken. The referee then decides which action to take, such as handing out a penalty.

In American football, one referee is responsible for watching the game. He is assisted by up to six other referees who have specific jobs. A line judge watches to see if the ball goes out of bounds and determines where the ball should be placed when the play starts. Other judges include the side judge, the back judge, the game judge, and the umpire.

The Football Field

Football is played on a rectangular field that is 100 yards long and 160 feet wide. At each end of the field, there is a section that measures 10 yards long. This is called the end zone. Lines that run across the field parallel to the goal line are called yard lines. They are labeled every 10 yards, from 0 to 50, or midfield on each side of the field. Yard lines help measure how far the football has moved on the field and establish the line of scrimmage.

Hash marks are two sets of short lines that run down the left and right side of the field. They mark single yards and help show where the ball should be placed when starting a play. Each play in football starts between or on the hash marks.

The line that separates the main field from the end zone is called the goal line. Goalposts are positioned on the back line of each end zone. They look like a large letter H.

In 2009, plans were made for major renovations to the Rose Bowl Stadium.

The grass on the field can be made up of real sod or a humanmade product called **turf**. Real grass does not stand up as well under the wear and tear of the game. Some stadiums are indoors, so grass is harder to grow. In these places, turf is used instead.

Players on the Team

A football team has 11 offensive and defensive players on the field at one time. The offense consists of the quarterback, linesmen, backs, tight ends, and receivers. The defense is made up of defensive ends and tackles, cornerbacks, and safeties. The quarterback gets the ball from the snap, decides plays, and passes the ball to receivers or running backs. Running backs run with the ball to gain a small number of yards. Wide receivers catch passes. The center, offensive guards, offensive tackles, and tight ends are blocking positions. They make sure that the quarterback and receivers can move the ball without the other team's defensive players stopping them. Defensive ends stop the quarterback from throwing the ball or running with it. Defensive tackles, nose guards, and linebackers try to keep the offense from gaining any yards. Cornerbacks and safeties keep the opposing team from catching passes and scoring touchdowns. Other players on a team include the kicker and **punter**.

THE FOOTBALL FIELD

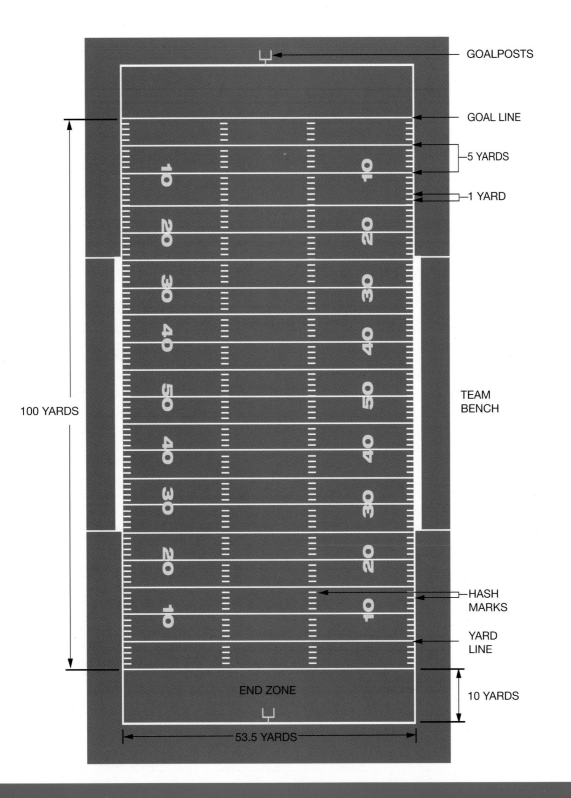

Football Equipment

Football players run into each other with a great deal of speed. They do this to try to stop the other team from moving down the field and into the end zone or so that their own teammates can move the ball ahead. These heavy hits can cause major injuries. Special gear is worn to protect the players' bodies from injury.

One of the most important pieces of equipment is the helmet. Helmets are made of hard plastic. They are lined with air cushions to help soften a hit to the head from other players or from the ground. Helmets also have metal bars to protect the face.

Helmet

Shoulder pads

Jersey

Gloves

Cleats

Shorts

Socks

GET CONNECTED

For more information about football uniforms past and present, visit **http://footballuniform history.com**.

Shoulder pads

Shoulder pads protect the player's neck and collarbone. They are made of hard plastic and are lined with foam. Each position wears different shoulder pads. Some, such as linebackers, have big pads because they take more hits than other players. Receivers wear lightweight pads so they can run faster and catch the ball more easily.

Thigh, knee, hip, tailbone, rib, and elbow pads help protect the players when they get hit or tackled by the opposing team. Players also wear mouth guards to keep their teeth from being damaged during the rough play of the game.

Mouth guard

Some players wear special gloves to help them hold onto the football. Most players wear special football shoes, called cleats, that help them grip the field and keep from slipping on the grass or turf. Cleats have flat-tipped spikes on the bottom.

Cleats

Team Uniforms

College football uniforms come in many colors. Teams most often wear the same colors as those used by the university the team represents. This helps **spectators** tell opposing teams apart during a game. Players usually wear a tight shirt with short sleeves. Each player's name and number are written on the shirt, along with the team name or logo. Football players wear tight pants, making it more difficult for players to pull each other to the ground. The pants are cut off just below the knee. Players always wear their helmets as part of their uniforms.

Qualifying to Play

Before 1946, Rose Bowl games were played between a team from the Pacific Coast Conference (PCC) and a team from one of the eastern states. Neither team had to be the champions of their conference or state. After 1946, the rules changed slightly. A team from the Pacific Coast Conference was pitted against a team from one of the "Big-10" universities in the midwestern and eastern states. However, this still typically resulted in a team from the west coast playing a team from the east.

During World War II, many teams had to withdraw from qualifying for the Rose Bowl. Many of their players had stopped attending university to fight in the war instead. Other players took regular jobs to help with the shortage of workers caused by the number of men fighting in the war. Some teams did not have enough players to field a team.

The United States entered World War II in 1941. As a result, the army recommended the Rose Bowl be postponed. It was concerned that a large gathering of people on the west coast would be a target for an attack.

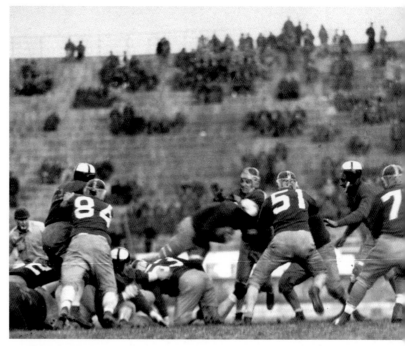

During World War II, the army and air force held football games for the men fighting in the war.

Some colleges continued to play during the war, but special rules were put in place to help teams whose players had gone to war.

Duke University and Oregon State were scheduled to play in the Rose Bowl in 1942. Instead of canceling the game, Duke invited Oregon to play at its stadium in North Carolina instead.

In 1998, the Rose Bowl became part of the Bowl Championship Series. There are four bowl games played across the United States each year as a playoff series. This helps to determine the national champion team. Even as part of this playoff series, the organizers of the Rose Bowl still try to keep up the tradition of hosting a competition between a team from the west and a team from the east.

Early footballs were made of inflated pig bladders, giving the ball the commonly used term "pigskin." However, the modern football is made of paneled leather surrounding an inflated rubber pouch.

Pac-10 Conference

The Pacific Coast Conference was formed in 1916 with four teams. The conference became the Pacific 8 Conference in 1968, when four more teams joined. It then became the Pacific 10 (Pac-10) in 1978. The Rose Bowl has been in association with the Big 10 and Pac-10 Conferences since 1946. Often, the champion of the Big 10 Conference plays the champion of the Pac-10 Conference on January 1 in Pasadena each year. Pac-10 members are the University of Southern California, University of Oregon, Oregon State University, University of California, University of Arizona, Arizona State University, Stanford University, Washington State University, University of Washington, and University of California, Los Angeles.

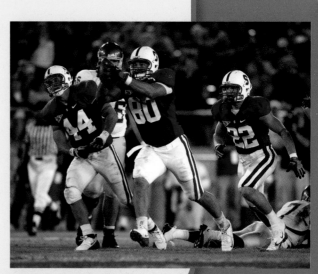

Where They Play

There are more than 100 varieties of rose bushes between the stadium and the fence around it.

Until 1922, all of the Rose Bowl games were played at California's Tournament Park in Pasadena. The land for a stadium was purchased by the city of Pasadena in 1897, but construction did not begin until 1921. In 1922, the Rose Bowl Stadium was completed, and the 1923 game was played there. The stadium cost $272,198 to build. Seat subscriptions bought by 210 individuals and companies paid for the costs.

Tournament Park held about 43,000 people. When it was first built, the Rose Bowl Stadium held 57,000 people. Today, more than 92,500 people can be seated inside the stadium.

The Rose Bowl Stadium measures 880 feet (268 m) in length from the north to south rims, and 695 feet (212 m) wide from the east to west rims.

The U.S. National Register of Historic Places has named the Rose Bowl Stadium a National Historic Landmark. Though it is known mainly for the New Year's Tournament of Roses football game, five National Football League Super Bowl games have been played there. It also is home to the UCLA Bruins college football team of the Pacific Coast Conference. In addition, the 1994 Men's World Cup of soccer, the 1999 Women's World Cup of soccer, the 2002 and 2006 Bowl Championship series games, and the 1932 and 1984 Olympic soccer matches were played at the Rose Bowl Stadium.

It would take about 84,375,000 gallons (319,394,138 liters) of water to fill the Rose Bowl Stadium to the rim.

ROSE BOWL FINAL SCORES				
YEAR	WINNING TEAM	SCORE	LOSING TEAM	SCORE
1999	Wisconsin	38	UCLA	31
2000	Wisconsin	17	Stanford	9
2001	Washington	34	Purdue	24
2002	Miami	37	Nebraska	14
2003	Oklahoma	34	Washington State	14
2004	USC	28	Michigan	14
2005	Texas	38	Michigan	37
2006	Texas	41	USC	38
2007	USC	32	Michigan	18
2008	USC	49	Illinois	17
2009	USC	38	Penn State	24

Mapping Rose Bowl Winners

USC - 2004, 2007, 2008, 2009

Oklahoma - 200

Texas - 2005, 2006

Many teams have had the honor of playing in the Rose Bowl since the first game in 1902. This map shows the locations of the winning teams from 1999 to 2009.

Winning Teams from 1999 to 2009

Miami   USC

Oklahoma   Washington

Texas   Wisconsin

N
W — E
S

Scale

621 Miles

0   1,000 Kilometers

Wisconsin - 1999, 2000

Washington - 2001

Miami - 2002

Women in Football

Women's football has a long history in the United States. In 1926, one of the first organized games was played when the Frankford Yellow Jackets hired women to play during halftime at their games. Since that time, there have been many women's football events. In fact, there are **semi-professional** and **amateur** leagues all over the country. In some cases, women even are allowed to play on men's teams.

The Women's Professional Football League (WPFL) was formed in 1965 by a businessman named Sid Friedman. Nine years later, the National Women's Football League (NWFL) was established. Though the leagues enjoyed some success in the beginning, over time, people lost interest in their games.

Today, there are several women's football leagues in the United States. They include the Independent Women's Football League (IWFL), the National Women's Football Association (NWFA), the Women's Football League (WFL), and the Women's Professional Football League (WPFL). The Women's Football Alliance is a new league that began in 2009. There are 38 teams in this league. All of these leagues hold their own championship games.

GET CONNECTED

Check out the Independent Women's Football League to learn more about women's football.
www.iwflsports.com

The Detroit Demolition had a 52-game winning streak between the 2002 and 2006 seasons.

The WPFL has 15 teams in cities across the country, including Houston, New York, and Los Angeles, as well as seven **expansion** teams. The WPFL was formed in 1999, when two entertainment promoters, Carter Turner and Terry Sullivan, started organizing woman's exhibition games in places such as the Hubert H. Humphrey Metrodome in Minneapolis, Minnesota. They even held an all-star game at the Orange Bowl in Miami, Florida.

During the week of Super Bowl XXXIV, the National Football League (NFL) invited WPFL to play an exhibition game. The Dallas Diamonds won three WPFL titles in a row from 2004 to 2006.

The Detroit Demolition have won the IWFL Championship five times.

In addition to professional and semi-professional organizations, girls can play **touch football** and **flag football** in many different leagues. In some cases, boys and girls play on the same teams. There also are girls-only teams that play full-contact, tackle football. Sometimes, high schools allow girls to play tackle football with the boys on their community or school teams.

Women's Football Leagues

The IWFL began in 2000. About 1,600 women play in this league in both the United States and Canada. The league is made up of 41 teams, and it has a championship game each year. In 2009, the IWFL will take part in a bowl game called the Pink Ribbon Bowl.

Historical Highlights

The Rose Bowl has become an icon of American college football. As the bowl game with the longest history, it has had many significant historical moments.

The first Rose Bowl played in the official Rose Bowl stadium, in 1923, was a match between the University of Southern California (USC) and Pennsylvania State University (Penn State). Though it was the ninth Rose Bowl, it was the first appearance at the event for both teams. USC won 14 to 3, but the low-scoring game was not a very exciting way to introduce the new stadium. In fact, the entire last quarter of the game was played without either team scoring a point.

In 1947, the University of California, Los Angeles (UCLA) and Illinois University faced off in the Rose Bowl. Illinois beat UCLA by a score of 45 to 14. During the game, UCLA's Al Hoisch had a **kick return run** of 103 yards (94 m). This still stands as the longest-kick return in Rose Bowl history.

In the 1995 Rose Bowl, Oregon played Penn State. Oregon's Danny O'Neil broke five Rose Bowl records during that game.

The 2005 Rose Bowl was the first time a Big-10 Conference champion did not face a team from the Pacific-10 Conference. Michigan University played the University of Texas. Texas kicked the ball through the **uprights** just as the fourth quarter ended, winning the game by a single point. This was the first time these two teams had faced one another, even though both teams had been playing for many years.

The University of Texas played in the Rose Bowl again in 2006. That year, its opponents were the USC Trojans. Both teams had very strong regular seasons leading up to the Rose Bowl. Again, the game was close right into the final 10 seconds. Vince Young of Texas scored a last-minute touchdown to give USC its first Rose Bowl loss since 1989.

Only four players in Rose Bowl history have been named MVP more than once. Charles White was given this title in 1979 and 1980.

ROSE BOWL MVPs 1999 to 2009		
NAME	TEAM	YEAR
Mark Sanchez	USC	2009
John David Booty (Offense) & Rey Maualuga (Defense)	USC	2008
Dwayne Darrett (Offense) & Brian Cushing (Defense)	USC	2007
Vince Young (Offense) & Michael Hull (Defense)	Texas	2006
Vince Young	Texas	2005
Matt Leinart	USC	2004
Nate Hybl	Oklahoma University	2003
Ken Dorsey & Andre Johnson	Miami	2002
Marques Tuiasosopo	Washington	2001
Ron Dayne	Wisconsin	2000
Ron Dayne	Wisconsin	1999

LEGENDS
and Current Stars

Wallace Wade – Back

Wallace Wade played college football for Brown University. In 1923, he began a prestigious career coaching college football, baseball, and basketball for the University of Alabama and Duke University. Wade led the Alabama team to the Rose Bowl in 1925, 1926, and 1930. The Rose Bowl of 1942 was held at Duke University in North Carolina. In 1967, the stadium at this university was renamed in Wade's honor. Wade was inducted into the Rose Bowl Hall of Fame in 1990.

Warren Moon

Warren Moon – Quarterback

Warren Moon began his college football career playing quarterback for the University of Washington Huskies. He helped the Huskies get to the 1978 Rose Bowl, which they won despite being the **underdog** team. Moon was named Most Valuable Player (MVP) of that Rose Bowl match-up. He then went on to play in both the Canadian Football League (CFL) and the National Football League (NFL). Moon set many football records. These records were not broken for years after Moon retired from playing football. He was inducted into the Rose Bowl Hall of Fame in 1997.

Dick Butkus

Dick Butkus – Linebacker

Dick Butkus played for the University of Illinois from 1962 to 1964. He is considered one of the best players of his generation. Butkus was inducted into the Rose Bowl Hall of Fame in 1995. He also is in the Pro Football Hall of Fame. The Dick Butkus Award is given out each year to the most outstanding linebacker in college football.

Sam Bradford – Quarterback

Sam Bradford began playing for the Oklahoma Sooners in 2007. In his first season as starting quarterback, he broke many records and was named Sporting News Freshman of the Year. The following year, Bradford received many more honors, including the Heisman Memorial Trophy for 2008. This is considered the most prestigious award for the top collegiate football player.

Sam Bradford

Famous Firts

The Rose Bowl game played on January 1, 1947, was the first "modern day" Rose Bowl game. The 1947 game pitted the champions of the Pacific-10 Conference against the champions of the Big-10 Conference.

The first Rose Bowl game played as a Bowl Championship Series (BCS) game was played on January 1, 1999. It was between Wisconsin and UCLA. Wisconsin won, with a score of 38 to 31.

In 2002, the Rose Bowl was not played by the champions of a Pacific-10 or a Big-10 team for the first time since 1919. When the Rose Bowl became part of the Bowl Championship Series, teams from different conferences could play in the Rose Bowl. In 2002, the Miami Hurricanes played the Nebraska Cornhuskers for the title that year.

USC Trojans quarterback Mark Sanchez led his team to win the 95th Rose Bowl against the Penn State Nittany Lions.

At the Rose Bowl in 2009, the University of Southern California became the first team to win three straight Rose Bowls. Led by Mark Sanchez, USC won with a score of 38 to 24 over Pennsylvania State University. Sanchez, USC's quarterback, set a Rose Bowl **pass completion** record. Eighty percent of the passes he threw were caught by USC players.

In 2009, the USC Trojans had their 24th Rose Bowl win.

Bowl Championship Series

In the early 1990s, the Bowl Coalition formed. It was made up of five conferences, as well as one individual team—Notre Dame. The coalition took part in six bowl games each year, not including the Rose Bowl. Before this time, teams signed contracts to take part in specific bowl games. This meant they could not play in others. Under the new agreement, teams could play in any of the bowl games if it meant that a clear winner could be determined. However, many teams, including those contracted to play in the Rose Bowl, are not part of the agreement. This means that, if one of the top-ranked teams is from Big-10 or Pac-10, it cannot take part in a national championship game. As a result, some years could pass without a clear national champion. The Bowl Alliance formed in the mid-1990s and included four conferences with three bowl games. However, it still did not include the Pac-10 or Big-10 teams. The Bowl Championship Series began in 1998, and the Rose Bowl Association agreed to let its teams take part if needed. The BCS helps to show off college football and its star players. The Rose Bowl will host the BCS national championship game again in 2010. This will be the third time it has done so since 1998.

The Rise of the Rose Bowl

1890

The first Tournament of Roses celebration takes place.

1900

The first bowl game, called the East–West game, is played at the Tournament of Roses.

1902

The first Rose Bowl game is played. It is not played again for 14 years.

1916

The Rose Bowl returns to the Tournament of Roses.

1923

The Rose Bowl game is played in the Rose Bowl Stadium for the first time.

1942

The Rose Bowl game is moved to Duke University in North Carolina because of World War II attack threats.

1947

The Rose Bowl sells out its tickets for the first time and every year after.

2009

The Pennsylvania State University Nittany Lions play the University of Southern California Trojans in the Rose Bowl. The Trojans win their third Rose Bowl in a row.

1989

The Rose Bowl celebrates its 75th anniversary.

1998

The Rose Bowl becomes part of the Bowl Championship Series.

1952

The Rose Bowl is the first college football game to be broadcast nationally.

1953

The Rose Bowl Player of the Game Award is created.

1973

A record crowd of 106,869 people attend the Rose Bowl.

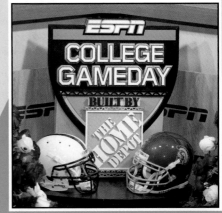

QUICK FACTS

- The Rose Bowl has showcased 18 Heisman Memorial Trophy winners. This trophy is given to the Most Outstanding College Football player.

- The Rose Bowl has honored 95 college football legends, inducting them into the Rose Bowl Hall of Fame.

Test Your Knowledge

1 What year was the first Rose Bowl game played?

2 How long is a football game?

3 How many players are on the field at one time for a team?

7 What city does the Tournament of Roses take place in?

8 What was the one year that the Rose Bowl did not take place in Pasadena?

9 What is the name of the first stadium in Pasadena that was used for the Rose Bowl?

10 Who played the first game at the Rose Bowl Stadium in 1923?

4 What position is responsible for throwing or running with the ball when the play starts?

5 What is the highest attendance at a Rose Bowl game?

6 What Rose Bowl legend has a stadium in North Carolina named after him?

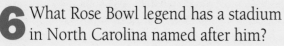

Answers: 1.) 1902 2.) There are four quarters in a game of football. Each quarter is 15 minutes in length. It takes about three hours to play four 15-minute quarters. 3.) eleven players 4.) quarterback 5.) 106,869 people in 1973 6.) Wallace Wade 7.) Pasadena, California 8.) 1942 9.) Tournament Park 10.) USC and Penn State

Further Research

If you are interested in learning more about American football, in particular, the Rose Bowl, you can find information in a variety of different places. Books and the Internet will always be your best bet when you want to learn more about a subject. You can borrow books from a library in your area or surf the Net.

Books to Read

Your local library is sure to have many books with information about the Rose Bowl and American football in general. By entering some information into their database computers, you will be able to locate the books that will help you learn more about your topic of choice.

Online Sites

For a great deal of the information about the Rose Bowl Stadium, visit **www.rosebowlstadium.com**.

The Tournament of Roses has its own website at **www.tournamentofroses.com**.

To learn about professional American football, visit **www.nfl.com**.

Find information about the Pacific 10 Conference and the Big Ten Conference at **www.pac-10.org/sports/m-footbl/pac10-m-footbl-body.html** and **http://bigten.cstv.com/sports/m-footbl/big10-m-footbl-body.html**.

Glossary

amateur: a person who is not paid to play a sport

bowl game: a post-season college football game

conference: an association of teams that play against one another

defensive: the team that is trying to keep the opposition from scoring on their end of the field

expansion: when a new team is added to a professional sport league

flag football: a type of football in which players are downed by having a flag pulled from their uniform

foul: an unfair act

kick return run: to catch a ball from a kickoff and attempt to run it in the opposite direction

offensive: the team that has the ball and is attempting to score on the opposition

pass completion: a successful forward pass

punter: a player who drops the ball from his or her hands and kicks it before it touches the ground

retroactively: to take effect from a date in the past

semi-professional: to play a sport for money but not as a full-time career

snap: putting the football into play by throwing the football between the player's legs, backwards from the line of scrimmage to the waiting quarterback or other player

spectators: people who are watching an event take place live

touch football: a type of football in which players are downed by touching them

turf: a layer of matted earth, held together by grass and grass roots; artificial turf is synthetic or carpet-like materials made to look like grass, used as a surface for football fields

underdog: the team that is expected to lose the game

uprights: posts that extend upright from the goalpost

Index

Bradford, Sam 25
Butkus, Dick 25

Duke University 15, 24, 28

equipment 12, 13

Heisman Memorial Trophy 25, 29

Leishman Trophy 5

Moon, Warren 24

referees 9
rules 5, 8, 9, 14

Sanchez, Mark 4, 23, 26, 27

touchdown 4, 8, 9, 10, 23
Tournament of Roses 4, 5, 6, 7, 17, 28, 30, 31

USC 4, 17, 18, 19, 22, 23, 26, 27, 29, 30

Wade, Wallace 24, 30